Burren

County Clare
By Maryangela Keane

Introduction and Description

The name Burren comes from Gaelic, it means 'a rocky place'. Historically the name Burren referred to the Barony of Burren situated in north-west County Clare. Geographically, the name has a far wider and more complex sense and meaning. The Burren area extends some 40.2 km from east to west, and 32.2 km from north to south. It lies between Galway Bay on the north, the Atlantic coast on the west and a line drawn roughly through Doolin, Kilfenora, Gort and Kinvara. However, there is some characteristic 'Burren' outside this area to the east where one can find the same features, but perhaps not as frequently or as concentrated. The Burren is a gently sloping carboniferous limestone landscape (**1**), broadly dissected by numerous joints running north to south. It is the youngest landscape in Europe and has suffered intense glaciation, the last occurred as recently as about 10,000 years ago.

In the Burren one can observe almost all the typical limestone landforms; underground rivers, swallow holes, glacial erratics, caves, clints, grykes and closed depressions (turloughs). This limestone is an organic sedimentary rock laid down millions of years ago in a shallow warm sea, it is the result of marine plants and animals dying and accumulating in horizontal beds on the sea floor. The limestones of the northern Burren are almost horizontal and dip only very gently to the south but in the south-eastern Burren the limestones are gently compressed into open folds, as is particularly well seen at Mullaghmore (627 ft). This mountain (**2**) illustrates both anticlinal and synclinal folding and the way in which the two different fold types react to weathering and erosion. In the anticlinal, the joints have become expanded and the beds stretched, therefore erosive agents can enter the rocks more easily; whereas in the synclinal the joints and the beds are compressed, and tighter, and rather squashed looking. At the foot of the mountain, there is a polje or closed depression, locally known as a turlough.

Turloughs (Dry Lakes)

These are grassy hollows, sometimes extending over many acres. which during wet weather fill with water through subterranean passages in the rock and empty by the same means. The rate of the rise and fall and the duration and frequency of the flooding varies in different turloughs, being dependent on several factors connected with underground drainage. These changes are in many cases quite rapid; an appreciable amount of water can collect in one hour, and disappear in an equally short time. Some turloughs hold permanent water on their floors, others show no water at all when flooding is absent, the bottom as well as the sides being covered with a rich green sward. Swallow holes set among the muddy moss-covered rocks often indicate the point of inflow and outflow.

Limestone Pavements, Clints, Grykes and other micro forms

As the ice-cap moved into the Burren from the north-east it carried with it some debris, such as the granite boulders (Glacial erratics) on the coast line. However, the main action of the glacier was to scour the rock clean of any superficial cover that formerly may have lain on the surface, thus exposing and smoothly polishing the underlying bedrock which we know today as the largest classic karst limestone pavements in these islands. Pavements are made up of two separate but integral parts known as clints and grykes. Clints are the blocks of limestone that constitute the paving, their area and shape is directly dependent upon the frequency and pattern of grykes. Grykes are the fissures that isolate the individual clints. The most dominant gryke system runs almost north to south and there is a secondary less-developed system at right angles to it (**4** and **5**). Grykes can stretch for hundreds of feet until they suddenly terminate or are lost beneath superficial deposits. Grykes are usually straight but are occasionally curvilinear.

Water is the dynamic of the Burren, water created it, and water is destroying it. This destruction can be seen in some of the clints where the water draining from the horizontal top is cutting deep channels or **runnels** into the shoulders of the clint, thus directing the water into the gryke where it will eventually widen the gryke and undermine the clint itself. On some clint tops one will see small saucer shaped depressions or **shallow pans**. These pools hold water, and can hold a layer of organic material, which includes algae called Nostoc. This algae exudes a mild acid which further breaks down the limestones, and so an even larger depression is formed which will eventually hold a colony of soil capable of sustaining a disparate assemblage of plants and grasses.

Forest Clearance and the Coming of Early Man

Climatic changes in post-glacial time have probably played a part in the destruction of vegetation cover, especially the trees over the high Burren. But it is only a minor role compared to that played by man and his activities. There is nothing to indicate large expanses or bare pavements before forest clearance by man. During the Boreal and Atlantic periods the pollen diagrams suggest a more or less complete cover of pine with hazel and yew. With the advent of agriculture, pine decreased steadily in importance, and in the early centuries of our era it had been replaced by a mixed woodland of oak, ash, elm and hazel. Clearly neither the present bare limestone and grassland nor hazel or ash woodland of the kind now found in the Burren represents the natural state of affairs. Under suitable conditions, recovery of bare eroded limestone pavements could take

6

place relatively quickly as for example in the deep cliff-sided valley of Glencurran which is now so thickly wooded that progress is difficult. In this wood there do not seem to be any trees of great age and opinion is that they have all grown up within the last hundred years. Yet the canopy is so thick that there is grass only in the open glades. Man has inhabited the Burren for some 6000 years, other than we know that these early people were cattle graziers we do not have any evidence of his living habits, however we do have his graves. By and large the most outstanding field monument from that period is the Portal Dolmen at Poulnabrone (**6**). It is one of the four of this type in the area. It dates from c.3600 BC and faces north-north-east, tapering to the south-south-west. The capstone measures 12 ft by 7 ft and rests lightly on the sidestones, it has its heavier end towards the front of the tomb where two tall portal stones give it a monumental appearance. As it stands now, it is a mere skeleton of its former self. It may have originally been covered by a cairn (loose stones and soil) which would have tapered to the back. A recent excavation revealed the burial system was by disarticulation and inhumation. The finds included unburnt disarticulated remains of between 16 and 22 adults also 6 juveniles. It was estimated on the meagre demographic data that the majority of the adults died before reaching the age of thirty with the exception of one that reached forty.

Wedge-shaped Gallery Graves (7)
These graves are very much more common in the Burren and at least 130 of them have been mapped and recorded. However, there are several others. They can occur in groups of two or three such as at Gleninsheen which date from 1500 BC. These box-like structures face into the west and taper to the east. They usually have two sidestones and one capstone. Sometimes they have two front stones – one permanent, the other movable to allow

the burial. One back stone achieved full closure. They have been stripped of their former covering and would probably have had large flagstones, set on edge around the grave in a railing-like fashion. A cairn would have covered the whole structure, burial was by cremation. The Burren has attracted settlers from every successive culture that arrived in Ireland since habitation began. Limestone terrain is remarkably poor in the preservation of organic remains. Conversely, it is the available abundance of stone that has helped to preserve the multiple field monuments from being used as a source of building material in later times. Robinson's map records thousands of sites from the Mesolithic, Neolithic, Celtic, Christian and medieval periods which demonstrate how man has altered the landscape, not only with roads and stone walls, but also with the many constructions indicative of where he lived, fought, woshipped and was buried. There must have been a great concentration of habitation in the Burren as the 1500 or so stone forts (Cahers and Cashels) (**14**) and a couple of earthen raths scattered throughout the area can testify. Most of these are obviously of a domestic nature but some such as Ballykinvarga with its defensive surrounding 'chevaux de frise' must have been extremely important as was Cahercommaun, a triple-ramparted fort sited on the edge of a vertical cliff. The fort at Cahermacnaghten has a diameter of 100 ft and was one of Ireland's most famous law schools, run by the O'Davoren family where the old Irish Behon Laws were taught. Oughtmama (**15**) was the site of the early monastic settlement founded by the three Colemans. Three churches remain.

The glorious twelfth century endowed the 'Burren' with innumerable field monuments, three of which are magnificent; Corcomroe Abbey in the north, Kilfenora in the south, and Dysert O'Dea east of

Kilfenora. The last two sites have fine High Crosses.

Dysert O'Dea (8, 10, 12)

This multiple site is about 4.8 km due south of Corofin. The church and the round tower stand on the site of an early Christian monastery founded by eighth century St. Tola. Where the church stands there was twelfth-century Romanesque nave-and-chancel church. This fell into decay, possibly in the seventeenth century, when the building was constructed in its present form and the Romanesque doorway with its beautifully carved human masks was inserted into the south wall. This doorway as again restored at a later date. It is now thought that some of these masks may have come from other Churches and were reassembled here in this grandiose style. Among them are four animal-type heads with a scroll going through their mouths. Perhaps these heads should have been placed together making a smaller circlet? High in the field to the east of the church is a fine twelfth-century High Cross, with a representation of a Christ triumphant and a bishop, possibly St. Tola. At the base of the cross is a handsome though weathered panel of four people, possibly representing the reform in the Irish church. This cross was restored and re-erected at least twice, once by Conor O'Dea in 1683, and secondly by the Synges in 1871. This family owned the red-brick house, the remains of which can be seen at the low end of the field to the west of the church and round tower.

Kilfenora Cathedral and High Crosses (9, 11)

The Catholic diocese of Kilfenora is famous in having the Pope as its bishop. The ancient cathedral is on the site of a sixth-century monastery founded by St. Factna, who is the patron saint of the village. It is a twelfth-century building, part of which is still used for divine worship. The roofless chancel of the church has a handsome three-lancet east window with interesting figures carved on the capitals.

The chancel is decorated by some

thirteenth- and fourteenth-century representations of Bishops and there is a handsome trefoil sedilia in the north wall. There are three complete and three shafts of beautiful twelfth-century High Crosses in Kilfenora. The most lavishly decorated one is the Doorty Cross (**11**) showing three different croziers, an Irish one, a continental style and a tau cross. On the west face which has weathered considerably there is a figure of Christ and a panel which has a representation of the entry of Christ into Jerusalem. West of the church, in the next field, is a very tall High Cross, again with a triumphant Christ figure and some intricate geometric and interlacing motifs. Another cross was removed to Killaloe in 1821 where it may be seen inside the door of the cathedral.

Lemeneagh Castle (13)
This is an O'Brien Tower House built in 1480, the eastern side is similar in construction to the many others throughout the Burren. However, in the seventeenth century this one had a massive fortified manor house built on to what was now considered to be an inconvenient tower. This added building has four storeys, and the mullioned windows in the ground and first storeys have eight lights, six lights in

the next and three at the top. Originally the main road ran around the back of the castle. One of the most colourful characters to live in this house, and indeed in all of Clare, was Maire Ruadh, wife of Conor O'Brien. At the time of the Cromwellian invasion, General Ludlow who led the skirmish in which Conor perished spoke of the Burren as a countryside 'that has not enough earth to bury a man, not enough timber to hang him or enough water to drown him'.

Because of Conor's death Maire Ruadh could have had all her lands confiscated. She cleverly averted this disaster by marrying a Cromwellian officer. Tradition has it that, at a later date, she disposed of this husband with equal indifference.

FLORA

Introduction and Arrival

It is probably the flowers that have received most attention and recognition and thus caught the imagination, despite the vast complexity of natural history interests that meet in this strange-looking 971 sq. km. Very many theories have been promoted to explain the presence of these plants in such a place. Wind, birds, or early man have at times been held accountable or favourably mentioned, but it would seem that the theory based on a climatic and glacial change is the most trustworthy.

Before the last glaciation, the Burren enjoyed a warmer climate and tundra conditions obtained which supported the southern (Lusitanian) plant life. Then the ice sheet started to invade the area from the north-east, fingers of ice clawed their way forward, slowly moving and gradually melting, dropping debris and extending the zone of the northern flora (Hibernian). The ice retreated from this warmer climate bequeathing the unique legacy of northern and southern plants growing side by side.

It is very easy to be misled into thinking that the flora of the Burren consists of rarities alone. This is not so, the mystique lies in the assemblage of plants, the co-existence of quite different ecological species growing side by side in the same sward. There is also the harmonious cohabitation of plants at sea level, of species which at these latitudes would normally grow on high mountain tops. The Burren is a meeting place of species of very varied types of distribution, and there is nowhere in Europe where Mediterranean and arctic-alpine plants grow together in a similar way.

There are important differences between the wild flowers of Ireland and those of Britain. In the first place there are fewer species and evidence suggests that this is because Britain was separated from Ireland earlier than from the Continent. Consequently some of the European flowers which probably entered England from across the Channel, and are now to be commonly found all over Britain, somehow failed to cross the Irish Sea. A good example of an abundant limestone species of this kind is Small Scabious (*Scabiosa columbaria*).

are kept down by the constant winter grazing of the cattle.

(II) *Influence of the Gulf Stream*. This has the effect of providing the west coast with a warm, moist, 'soft' air stream which is the essential element for the survival of the southern species. The winter/summer temperature differential is very small.

(III) *Natural Heat of the Limestone*. Last, but certainly not least, these rounded, terraced hills absorb heat from the Atlantic and summer sunshine. They act as giant storage heaters. There is a

Maintenance and Transhumance

Acknowledging that the plants are here, and perhaps agreeing with the theory as to how they got here, there is little room for doubt as to the reasons why they remain and thrive on this limestone plateau.

(I) *High Light Density*. The lifestyle of the arctic-alpine plants is greatly dependent on the amount of light that they receive. In the Burren a very high degree of light is achieved by the reflections from the sea, from the naked limestone, and perhaps most important of all, this collective light is not depleted by any air pollution or overshading shrubbery, even the grasses

reverse ground temperature curve in operation here. It is warmer on the hillsides and high valleys in the winter than on the low-lying lands, this promotes grass growth during the winter. This last curious factor dominates the farming pattern in the Burren as much today as it has done for

thousands of years. Even today when there are so many technological advances made in farming, the system of wintering cattle on the high mountains has not been abandoned. To understand the system of 'winterages' one must think of the Swiss practice of transhumance, where the cattle are taken from the mountains when the first shows of winter arrive and are housed under the dwellings until the spring. In the Burren because of the reverse temperature curve, the cattle are put up on the mountains for the winter – usually early in November and they remain there until late April; in most cases they require no additional feeding such as hay, silage, or grain, before they are taken down to the low-lying pastures. One cannot but ask, 'Well what on earth do they eat?' 'Where do they get sufficient water?' These are understandable queries, but these hillsides are deceptive, especially if you look up at them from sea level, because then you are only looking at the succession of escarpments which are indeed bare and formidable. However, it is on the terraces or benches, in the hollows and depressions that the grass grows abundantly. If the viewer were on top of the mountains and looking down, one would get a completely different impression, as now all the terraces appear to blend into each other making a seemingly green grassy slope, the lush product of the summer months. The growth of grass continues throughout the winter for which the three previously men-

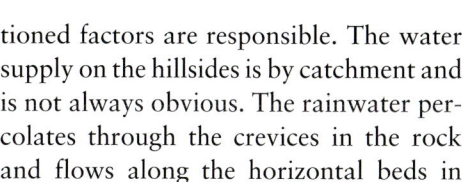

tioned factors are responsible. The water supply on the hillsides is by catchment and is not always obvious. The rainwater percolates through the crevices in the rock and flows along the horizontal beds in small streams to break out as small springs. After a short distance it disappears again and repeats the process by emerging a little further down and so on to each successive terrace.

FLOWER HUNTING

'Kissing is out of favour, when gorse is out of bloom'

The Burren is never out of bloom. Like one's own garden the plants here rotate with the seasons, and there is always something in bloom, be it a fern or moss in late autumn or winter right through to the spring and summer flora for which it is so well known.

It is of course in late May and June that the flower show is really 'on' in this exotic extensive rock garden that runs riot with colour. In such a huge area as this, people wonder 'where is the best place to go?' 'Where can I find the rare plants?' It is not the intention of this booklet to direct people to the most important stations for obvious reasons.

However, one need not feel 'left out' by that, because there are only one or two plants which are particularly scarce and need protection, and indeed it may be said that these are not among the most colourful or showy flowers. The aim is to make a trip to the Burren more rewarding and to explain a little of the background to whichever feature interests you, and hopefully encourage further study.

When one is hunting for what we have come to know as Burren Flora, it is best to avoid the obviously cultivated, fertilised farmland with deep soil pastures. Keep to the naked limestone, where the thin layer of soil is scantily stretched over the rocks. It is helpful to select an area where the grykes are fairly shallow allowing the all-important light to penetrate to the plants, yet deep enough to give them the shelter

26

they require. One does not have to climb to the very tops of the mountains to record any treasure, because the plants that grow there are also to be found at sea level or inland. For those who do venture to the top, there is the additional bonus of an

25

even more panoramic view of Galway Bay and the twelve Bens of Connemara.

Generally speaking some plants are more dominant and obvious than others even by their sheer numbers and growth pattern. It would be difficult to miss, or

not to be impressed by the sheets and sheets of **Mountain Avens (22)** (*Dryas octopetala*) that covers the terraced hills and act as a perfect backdrop for the rich blue **Spring Gentian (23)** (*Gentiana verna*). One cannot escape from the gleaming yellow of the **Hoary Rockrose (16)** (*Helianthemum canum*) interspersed here and there by the very small, dark blue, sometimes pink **Milkwort** (*Polagala vulgaris*). Even though we think of the orchids as being among the later species, the **Early Purple Orchid (31)** (*Orchis mascula*) is among the earliest plants, as is the **Burren Orchid (33)** (*Neotinea maculata*).

It is important to point out at this stage that should a visit not coincide with the main flowering period of the plants, there is still a chance of seeing a late straggler on a northern-facing slope and equally an early bloom on a southern aspect, the higher one goes the better, and one will very rarely be disappointed even if a visit occurs as early as March or as late as August. A look at the map will help here. July and August have their own rewards and it is difficult to put into words the colour of the Burren in high summer. This is orchid time, a family which has already been described. Now the snow-like dryas has given way to the yellow of Ladies Bedstraw (*Galium verum*) punctuated here and there by tussocks of Wild Thyme (*Thymus druceii*). These two plants are everywhere, on the hillsides, on the rocks, on the walls, in every corner and crevice, even tumbling down to the road. The Wild Thyme could be described as the most hospitable host in the area, because it is to that plant that most of the parasites are attracted, to name a few:

Lesser Dodder (*Cuscuta epithymum*), **Eyebright** (*Euphrasia salisburgensis*) and **Broomrape** (*Orabanche rubra*). These parasites plug themselves into the thyme and draw from it their own requirements, be it minerals or salts. Neither party seems to suffer from the intrusion.

Like the rest of us, some plant families and groups have more members than others. In the Burren, the geraniums and eyebrights would appear to be particularly well endowed, having seven or eight of each family well represented. Most of the geraniums are quite common in the fields and hedgerows, both on and off the limestone, but one cannot help noticing the prolific growth of the **Bloody Cranesbill** (**24**) (*Geranium sanguineum*). This flower, which usually grows in clumps, is magenta coloured, so presumably it derives its English name from the fruit it bears, which is a reddish long beak, and the fact that the deeply divided leaves can turn red as they die. For those who wish to make a deeper study of plant life, there is ample scope for doing so in this area, from the very simple families to the very complicated such as the **Eyebrights** (*Euphrasia*). These small erect wiry-stemmed flowers with white or violet petals and usually a yellow eye grow abundantly here and can be divided with difficulty into eight identifiable species. There are in addition some plants which are intermediate between two species.

The isolation of Ireland has resulted in a reduced flora, but there are still about 1,000 species of flowering plants and ferns. As already suggested some of the flowers will be seen almost without looking, others are small, minute and more habitat conscious.

Identification and Habitats

The best way for a beginner to learn how to find interesting plants and how to identify them is to go out on field excursions with a more knowledgeable guide. Then with constant, repetitive identification of even a few of the species that the site holds, very soon the beginner will extend his knowledge. The use of a full colour illustrated flora will help one to associate the parts of a plant with the relevant text.

Similarly a 'nose' for good localities is best acquired by imitation. Every species has a certain range of tolerance of conditions of soil and climate, and it follows therefore that extreme and specialised environments offer the best chance of finding the rarer species. Go for the driest spots or the wettest, the sunniest or the shadiest, the sea-shore or the acid bogland. The spread of fertiliser on grassland has reduced the incidence of the common wayside plants so it is best to keep to waste ground, disused quarries and gravel ridges.

Flora of the Turloughs (Dry Lakes)

The effect of the frequent flooding in the turloughs is to alter profoundly the character of the vegetation. A dense covering of plants still prevails, but its composition is different from that of the limestone pavements or the pastureland around. The contrast between the areas which are subject to flooding and those free from it is increased because intermittent inundation and the very light deposit of limy sediment produce a sward particularly beloved by herbivorous animals, large and small. The vegetation of the turloughs is usually nibbled to the last leaf, and all are much dwarfed. The most abundant plants are those which can best withstand submergence or grazing or both. There is a total absence of rushes, willows, alder and many other plants which one associates with marshes or wet ground. The close sward loses species after species as the depth below flood level increases. The violets in the turloughs show a tolerably regular zonation.

Viola stagnina is generally on or near the floor ascending the sides sometimes for a few feet where *V. canina* appears. This has a vertical range of about 6 ft. Then *V. riviniana* comes next, still often a couple of yards below the limit of shrub growth; and finally in the woods and adjoining, *V. reichenbachiana* grows luxuriantly. A great variety of conditions in regard to flooding undoubtedly prevails in different turloughs so that data relative to one would be applicable only partially to any other.

(16) Hoary Rockrose
(*Helianthemum canum*)
A small creeping shrub, dark green leaves, white on the underside. Yellow flowers with five petals on a weak stem. Very local on dry limestone pavements. May–July.

(17) Greater Butterwort
(*Pinguicula grandiflora*)
Stemless, oblong pale greenish-yellow leaves that are insectivorous with a tendency to curl in. Flowers are violet with five overlapping petals that have wavy margins. On northern-facing wet and dripping rocks. Very rare. July.

(18) Maidenhair Fern
(*Adiantum capillus veneris*)
Leaves are pale green and fan shaped on slender shining black stems. Local in grykes, often found nestling under the dead growth. Fairly widespread.

(19) Fairy Foxglove (*Erinus alpinus*)
A low perennial, small leaves, pink/purple flowers, grows on mortared walls and surrounding boulders. April–May.

(20) Dactylorhiza cruenta
ssp. **D. incarnata**
Long lanceolate leaves very heavily spotted on both the inside and outside, dark purple flowers also heavily blotched. Turloughs. June.

(21) Limestone Bugle
(*Adjuga pyramidalis*)
Erect, very small plant. Basal leaves very much larger than those at the top which are stemless. Softly hairy. Flowers pale violet-blue. Very rare.

(22) Mountain Avens (*Dryas octopetala*)
A low prostrate shrub, with creeping woody stems, oak-shaped dark green leaves, white underneath. Creamy-white flowers with classically eight petals, frequently twice that. Widespread on pavements. April–July.

(23) Spring Gentian (*Gentiana verna*)
A densely tufted plant with single flowering stems. Flowers with five petals are an intense blue with small white scales between the five petals. Found in dense groups or individual plants. Tends to close

up if sun is not shining. Abundant on limestone rocks. May–June.

(24) Bloody Cranesbill
(*Geranium sanguineum*)
Big plant with deeply divided leaves, stems hairy, magenta flowers, with five petals, abundant on limestone and grassy heaths. June–August.

(25) Bee Orchid (*Ophrys apifera*)
This orchid resembles a bumble bee. Tall spikes may have three to six blooms on each spike. Slender leaves are green in winter and wither when the flower develops. Dry banks. July–August.

(26) Pyramidal Orchid
(*Anacamptis pyramidalis*)
This orchid with deep magenta flowers in a short dense pyramidal spike, leaves lanceolate from the base, very common especially on sand dunes. July–September.

(27) Lesser Butterfly Orchid
(*Platanthera bifolia*)
Tall plant, flowers creamy white, faintly tinged green, spur very long and slender. Damp pastures and heaths. Frequent June–July.

(28) Dactylorhiza o'kellyii ssp. **D. fuchsii**
Pure white orchid, cylindrical in shape, dense flowers, clear leaves, very common grassy heaths, roadsides. July–August.

(29) Fragrant Orchid
(*Gymnadenia conopsia*)
As the name suggests it has the fragrance of clove, a tall plant with pale pink/reddish-purple loose flowers. Frequent in pastures, healthy grassland.

(30) Dactylorhiza majalis
Leaves darkish green, spreading, broad and tapered at both ends, often spotted on the upper side. Flowers mauve to deep reddish purple. Marshes, bogs and wet places. May–July.

(31) Early Purple Orchid
(*Orchis mascula*)
Flowers vary in colour from pale pink to deep magenta on a moderately dense

cylindrical spike with a curved spike. Widespread on limestone and grassland. Early April–June.

(32) Fly Orchid (*Ophrys muscifera*)
This plant resembles a fly, quite tall with four to seven flowers on each pale green spike, rarely all in bloom together. Infrequent and rare, on fairly sheltered grassy slopes that are not too dry. June–July.

(33) Irish Orchid (*Neotinea maculata*)
Few leaves, occasionally spotted, greenish-white flowers that never open out fully, in a dense narrow spike, rather small, faintly fragrant and usually found on grassy heaths, gravel ridges and sandy places. May–June.

(34) Spring Sandwort (*Minuartia verna*)
A small tufted perennial, leaves crowded and needle-like white flowers with five petals, high standing stamens. Common over the rocks. May–September.

(35) Shrubby Cinquefoil
(*Potentilla fruticosa*)
A medium-sized shrub with peeling bark, yellow flowers with five petals, leaflets toothed in wet places especially turloughs. This plant blooms twice, once in June and later in August.

(36) Fern, Moonwort (*Botrycium lunaria*)
Six pairs of fan-shaped segments surrounds the fertile spike which is usually taller. Sheltered sides of walls. May–August.

(37) Dark red Helleborine
Epipactis atrorubens)
Lanceolate leaves on a tall (15-30 cm) hairy stem. Dark red cup-shaped drooping flowers. Found on limestone pavements, can show slight differences in colour due to location. July–August.

(38) Burnet Rose (*Rosa spinosissima*)
An erect very bushy shrub, flowers single, creamy white, occasionally pink on a very thorny branch. Fruit black. In grykes and rocky places. May–June.

(39) Mossy Saxifrage
(*Saxifrage hypnoides*)
A low-growing cushion-shaped perennial. Leaves fine with the segment ending in a small bristle. Abundant white flowers on slender stems, clumps of this cover the sea-sprayed rocks. May–August.

(**40**) **Calystegia soldanella**
A low creeping plant with prostrate stems and kidney-shaped leaves rather fleshy. Flowers are bell shaped and single, pale pink, sometimes tinged with white. Sandy seashore. June–July.

(**41**) **Lady's Tresses** (*Spiranthes spiralis*)
Slender stem with white scented flowers in a single spirally twisted row forming a slender spike. Sandy ground near the sea. August–September.

Climate

The Burren shares a highly oceanic climate with other western districts of the British Isles. The rainfall varies around 50 in. (125 cm) a year and May is normally the driest month. Local statistics are not available, but a programme of meteorological observations was initiated in recent years by Miss E. M. Shaw. Her study shows that Fanore was about 0.5°C warmer than Ballyvaghan in the colder winter months, and Kilfenora about 1°C cooler throughout the year, partly due to its higher altitude. This study also shows that the mean annual rainfall at Ballyvaghan is about 65 in.; Fanore about 52 in.; Kilfenora about 57 in.; Corofin about 50 in. and Kinvarra 46 in.

With the exception of the odd year every decade or so, frost and especially snow are uncommon. It is the wind that is the dominant feature here and one cannot but be puzzled by the branches of the small trees and shrubs growing at right angles to their trunks. In these cases the wind has prevented the branches from growing on the windward side and all activity and branch protrusion is on the leeward side, giving this unbalanced appearance. Other plants also suffer from the high winds and adapt accordingly, i.e. Juniper (*Juniperus communis*). Although this can be a prostrate undershrub, in the Burren it grows almost horizontally, moulding itself into strange shapes to find every little bit of shelter.

Mineral Resources and Mining (42)

There is a long tradition of mining in north-west Clare. Several points on detailed maps show sites of lead and silver mining. Lead and silver deposits have been found in the west side of Slieve Carron and also north of Fisher Street in Doolin. Fluorspar is found throughout the Burren. This decorative amethyst stone was worked from the open-cast site at Kilweelran townland in the parish of New Quay during the 1960s until the shallow seam was exhausted. Since then a deeper seam has been located but has not been worked. Fluorspar is used commercially as a flux in metal smelting and in steel manufacture. Calcite used in the manufacture of cement and paints is found in areas of the Burren. This is a white crystalline mineral that grows in from both sides of the grykes, and may completely fill the fissure. Borings in the townland of Mortyclough near New Quay proved positive, but the subsequent open-cast mining has now been discontinued. For a great many years flagstones have been mined in the Moher area and the dressing of the stones has given good local employment. This highly attractive dressed stone is used extensively as paving around modern buildings, as well as for fireplaces and other relief features.

Of all the worked minerals in the Burren, the mining of the phosphate deposits at Doolin and at Noughaval (3.2 km north-east of Kilfenora) was the largest enterprise. Some mining at Noughaval and Doolin was open cast, but the underground mine at Doolin was by far the biggest. During the Second World War when the embargoes prevented the importation of this fertiliser, these two seams were worked and approximately 115,000 tons were raised.

Birds

Because of the lack of cover in the central Burren the main bird population is confined to the fringes. Sea and coastal birds are mostly on the west and northern shores. The woodland species frequent the eastern areas around Gort. Because the habitats are limited in the central Burren the range of birds is moderate. None the less, within a few days spent bird watching one could easily record up to 120 species ranging from the common to the nesting puffins (**43**) and choughs. Winter waders find refuge in the slobs around Ballyvaghan and Muckinish. Birds of prey also play their part – kestrels and sparrowhawks being quite common.

Fishing

Historically the sea has been a major component in the life of north-west Clare. Fishing has long been a tradition (and in famine times a lifeline) for the coastal villages. Gleninagh (**44**) (Glen of the Ivy), which is close to Ballyvaghan, was important as a base for the lobster and mackerel fisherman. It has a fine pier and sandy beach. Curraghs, light timber-framed boats covered with tarred canvas, were home-constructed and usually capable of taking four to six occupants. Doolin, north of Liscannor and fronted by Crab Island. Here is a small tidal pier which has been the traditional terminus of Aran Clare traffic. A full ferry service is available from Doolin during the summer months. Ballyvaghan has a tidal pier from which several boats operate. New Quay also has a pier and a plant for the cultivation and export of oysters.

Feral Goats

Herds of goats (**45**) may be seen wandering all over the Burren. At one time the goat was a most important animal for each household, providing both milk and meat. It is still a great treat to have kid for the main meal on Easter Sunday in these parts. Alarm has often been expressed at the number of these animals lest they should overcrop the plants. Actually the reverse is true as they tend to keep their grazing activities to the scrubland, and thus keep down the ever invasive hazel scrub, and so form an important part of the ecological balance.

Literary Burren

One could, all too easily, become totally absorbed by the natural history interests of the Burren and overlook the Burren's fine literary tradition. It was in the eastern Burren at Coole Park, near Gort, that Lady Gregory gathered about her the literati of the day. G. B. Shaw, Sean O'Casey, Douglas Hyde, and W. B. Yeats made his summer home for twelve years in the nearby sixteenth-century tower house, Thoor Ballylee. A tower set by a stream's edge.

This De Burgo tower, provided the setting for some of his best loved poems, 'The Winding Stair' and 'The Tower Poems'. Raftery, another earlier poet who lived nearby also appreciated the poetic beauty of this locality. In 1926 Yeats, when writing to Olivia Shakespeare said, 'We are at our tower and I am writing poetry as I always do here, and as always happens, no matter how I begin, it becomes love poetry before I am finished with it. As you see I have no news, for nothing happens in this blessed place, but a stray beggar or a heron.'

Yeats originally came into these parts on a walking tour with his friend Arthur Symonds. They stayed at Tullira Castle as guests of Edward Martyn, and here Yeats was introduced to Lady Gregory. Later, Yeats spent many holidays as a guest of Lady Gregory at Coole Park, and during those he first came to the tower. In 1916 he bought it from the Congested District Board for thirty-five pounds! He went to considerable trouble to restore the tower with the most suitable material and in his absence the building was supervised by Lady Gregory.

On a tablet inserted in the wall of the tower are these words

> 'I the poet William Yeats,
> With old millboards and sea green slates,
> And smithy work from the Gort forge,
> Restored this tower for my wife George,
> And may these characters remain,
> When all is in ruin once again.'

And it was 'all ruin once again' ... Happily the tower house and associated cottages have been beautifully restored and have among many other things, a fine bookshop, and for the inner-man ... an excellent teashop.

Coole Park

Coole Park was purchased by the Gregory family on their return to Ireland following service with the East India Company in 1768, and remained in their ownership up to 1928 when it was sold to the state. The owner at that time was Lady Augusta Gregory, already a legend in her lifetime as a dramatist, folklorist and co-founder with W. B. Yeats and Edward Martyn of the Abbey Theatre. Lady Gregory's love of Coole and of its 'seven woods' immortalised by Yeats, comes through again and again in her writings and those of her contemporaries. It is said that whenever she received a fee or royalty she planted another tree. The house itself, the birthplace of the Irish Literary revival, was demolished by the state in 1940. However, the Irish Wildlife and Forestry services have now taken over the estate and are restoring the grounds to their former glory. It is in the walled garden that one can find the best known tree in Ireland, the great copper beech which is known as the Autograph Tree; Lady Gregory invited her literary guests to carve their initials on the trunk. Augustus John, George Bernard Shaw, Sean O'Casey and, of course, W. B. Yeats are among the guests on record.

Kilmacduagh Round Tower (47)

A rich archaeological site some 4.8 km west of Gort, it has one of the finest collections of churches in Ireland. The most conspicuous feature is the excellently preserved Round Tower which leans to one side. Irish round towers were never lived in, but at times of attack refuge was sought here, both for the monks and their possessions. The attackers, however, quickly learnt to extract some of the massive stones from the base, a fire was lit and the

round tower made a perfect chimney, totally destroying its contents.

Beside the tower is the cathedral, of which the west gable, with its blocked-up flat-headed doorway from the eleventh or twelfth centuries is the earliest part. The rest of the nave dates from about 1200. In the fifteenth century a fine doorway with the head of a bishop above it was inserted in the south wall, and it was then that the west doorway was blocked up. It is likely that at the same period the two transepts were added, the west window inserted and the chancel rebuilt. Not far away in a field to the north, is St. John's Church, a small twelfth-century church with rounded and pointed windows. Further north is a two-storey Glebe house of military appearance (possibly the abbot's house) built in the thirteenth century though altered later, and now being restored. In a field to the north-west is O'Heyne's Church, built in the first half of the thirteenth century with a beautiful chancel arch supported by pillars with animal and floral decoration and two excellently carved east windows. Beside this church are the remains of another of uncertain date, but with a fifteenth-century window above the door. East of the cathedral and on the other side of the road is St. Mary's Church. The churches were plundered in the thirteenth century and after the reformation the monastery passed to Richard, second earl of Clanriekard. *(Harbison, National Monuments of Ireland)*

Caves

The characteristic Burren cave is approached through a pothole or stream swallow hole at the shale limestone junction. A dendritic pattern of high narrow winding canyon passages with streams on their floors is the typical ground plan. Dripstone forms are few and with strong bedding control, internal pitches (descents) are rare. Ailwee Cave is the only cave open to the general public and it has a history stretching back millions of years. Originally there was a river in it, then wild animals; bear pits with the claw marks of the bears can still be seen. It is situated 3.2 km south of Ballyvaghan.

Lisdoonvarna Spa

The Spa at Lisdoonvarna is still in use. It has been visited for medicinal treatments since the mineral waters were discovered in the middle of the nineteenth century. The reason for the Spa being here is directly due to the last glaciation failing to remove an area of overlying mineral rich shales from the north eastern elevation of Slieve Elva. The ground water, percolating through those mineral rich shales, picks up trace elements and emerges as mineral springs of the Iron, Sulphur, and Magnesia waters that service the Spa. The water is drunk hot or cold. Treatments in addition to the hot sulphur baths include wax baths, saunas and physiotherapy. Like all Spas, Lisdoonvarna offers an active social life, a pavilion-type building in the spa complex has a fine ballroom and a lovely cafe overlooks the Gowlaun river. The many hotels and guesthouses in the village are open from Easter to October.

Conservation Status of the Burren

The development plan for the County of Clare states 'it is intended that all items of historic, archaeological, scientific or other academic interest in the area shall be protected'. The conduct of these ideals lies with Duchas – The Heritage Service. Over the years the State has acquired a considerable area in the south-east Burren to conserve as a National Park. With the exception of that, the Burren is privately owned by individual farmers and as such much be respected at all times.

Code of Conduct

In the interests of preserving the Burren as a unique Nature Reserve, it is illegal to remove stone from the pavements or walls. Take care not to disturb the field monuments, and respect the entire built heritage. Do not dig up, or pick plants, avoid doing anything that would expose them to unwelcome attention, such as making an obvious path to them, or trampling on the vegetation around such a place. Leave nothing, take nothing but photographs.

Acknowledgements

I should like to thank Dr David Webb for reviewing my plant records, Dr Marjorie Sweeting and Dr E. K. Tratman for their geological guidance, Mr John Bowman and Dr Michael O'Connor for their photographs, and Dick and Nan Deegan for the many excursions.

Limestone pavements in the west of Ireland. Paul Williams.
Flowers of chalk and limestone. Edward Lousley.
Guide to the National Monuments of Ireland. Peter Harbison.
Flora of the Turloughs. R Lloyd Praeger.
An Irish Flora. Dr D. A. Webb.
The Burren Map. Tim Robinson.

© Jarrold Publishing and Maryangela Keane, 2006
Designed and produced by Jarrold Publishing, Norwich
Printed in Great Britain 8/06